20✱ Questions

for girls

ACKNOWLEDGMENTS

Editorial Director: Erin Conley

Designer: Jeanette Miller

Special thanks to Erin Anthony, Suzanne Cracraft, Peter Crowell and Kristen Schoen for their invaluable assistance.

© 2005 University Games

First edition published in 2005

Spinner Books, a division of

University Games Corporation
2030 Harrison Street San Francisco, CA 94110

University Games Europe B.V.
Australielaan 52 6199 AA Maastricht Airport, Netherlands

University Games Australia
10 Apollo Street Warriewood 2102 Australia

Library of Congress Cataloging-in-Publication Data on file with the publisher

ISBN: 1-57528- 984-9

Printed in China

1 2 3 4 5 6 7 8 9 10 – 09 08 07 06 05

CONTENTS

RULES 4

INTRODUCTION 6

PEOPLE 7

PLACES 57

THINGS 93

RULES

For 1 or more players!

OBJECT

◉ The object of the game is to show off your smarts by correctly guessing 10 well-known mystery topics.

STARTING THE GAME

◉ The youngest player spins the spinner and says, "I am a _____" (person, place or thing) as shown on the spinner. The youngest player then becomes that person, place or thing for the entire first round of play. This player acts solely as the Reader and may not play until the next round.

GETTING A CLUE

◉ The Reader must now flip to the start of the choosen category (i.e. person, place or thing) and read clue #1 aloud to the group.

◉ After listening to the clue, the player to the Reader's left (a.k.a. the Guesser) has 10 seconds to guess who/what the Reader is. (Players may only guess when it's their turn.)

◉ If the Guesser guesses correctly, s/he scores one point. The player to the Reader's right becomes the new Reader.

◎ If the Guesser guesses incorrectly, the player to his/her left gets the next clue and may then try to crack the 20 Questions case.

◎ Once all players have acted as the Reader, it is time to spin again! The player to the left of the last person to spin now spins to determine the type of category to be played. S/he is the first Reader for this round.

Tip: Even if it sounds silly, just take a guess. There is no penalty for an incorrect guess! And statistics show that you have no chance of winning if you don't make a guess.

WINNING THE GAME

◎ The first player to score 10 points wins the game!

PLAYING ON YOUR OWN

◎ Going solo? Good. You can be the Reader and the Guesser! Keep track of how many clues it takes to guess the correct answer. Guess eight topics correctly in less than 80 clues and you're a winner!

INTRODUCTION

Hi!

When you are the father of three girls and the president of a game company, there is a great deal of pressure to design fun products for your top fans. This book is specially developed for my three little (and growing) bundles of joy.

I have created **20 Questions for Girls** to be the type of book that can be read for ten minutes or two hours and picked up again and again. It has 1400 clues and covers more than 70 mystery topics, which should be familiar to almost all eight, nine and ten-year-old readers who haven't been hiding under a rock. The real trick is not in guessing the person, place or thing, but to guess as quickly as possible.

Every topic in the book is guaranteed to please and perplex, and has been kid-tested in my very own family lab (a.k.a. my living room). Here's how the testing works:

1. I enter the front door and my family barrages me with questions like
   "Guess who I am?" "Guess what I did?" and "Guess where I went today?"
2. I guess and guess and guess.
3. I hope that it will end and that I can sit down and have a cold drink.
4. My three daughters finally fill me in on the excitement in their lives.

Then I ask the girls to play my version of **20 Questions for Girls**, hoping to confound and confuse them. Alas, my plot rarely works. By the tenth clue the kids have usually figured out my conundrum and I am back to guessing about their exciting day. However, you can benefit from trying the puzzlers in this book and seeing if you can decipher the person, place or thing on each page as fast as the Moog kids.

Either way (fast or not so fast), have fun learning and playing!

—Bob

People

I am a Person

1. I've been around the world.
2. I am not American.
3. I was born in 1974.
4. I am full of character.
5. I'm not a designer, but I do decorate handbags and t-shirts.
6. I like to bake cookies.
7. I am from Japan, but am said to live in London.
8. I love pink!
9. Some people see me as a fashion statement.
10. I have no mouth, but I always say "Hello."
11. According to legend, I am the height of five apples and the weight of three.
12. I have a pet hamster named Sugar.
13. My image is plastered on everything from books to backpacks, toys to toasters.
14. I almost always have a bow or flower in my hair.
15. I have a twin sister named Mimmy.
16. I have my own pet cat, Charmmy Kitty.
17. Badtz-Maru, Chococat and Nyago are part of my crowd.
18. I am drawn in the kawaii style, which means "cute" in Japanese.
19. Sanrio™ makes me.
20. I am a cartoon character.

People

I AM HELLO KITTY.

I am a Person

1. I'm a Texan at heart.
2. I was born in 1982.
3. I used to be a waitress.
4. I'm used to being judged.
5. I think it's important to vote.
6. If we did karaoke, I'd probably be better than you.
7. I've been featured in a Got Milk? ad.
8. I joined the school choir at 13.
9. I like to sing my heart out.
10. You might have seen me on national TV.
11. I had to go through a lot of auditions to get to where I am.
12. People say I'm very down to earth.
13. I was nominated for three 2005 Video Music Awards.
14. I won a big contest.
15. I beat out Justin.
16. I am very *Thankful* for my fans.
17. There's a lot behind "These Hazel Eyes."
18. I know Randy, Paula and Simon.
19. A lot has happened "Since You've Been Gone."
20. I was the very first American Idol.

2

People

I AM KELLY CLARKSON.

I am a Person

1. I like to act, but it's not what I'm known for.
2. I live in Florida.
3. My father was my coach and manager.
4. I was born in 1981.
5. I'm very athletic.
6. When I'm at work, I'm not looking for love.
7. I do a lot of charity work for kids.
8. My Jack Russell terrier Jackie travels with me everywhere.
9. I share my last name with a funny Robin.
10. In my racket, you wear sneakers.
11. My older sister shares her name with a planet.
12. I won Olympic gold.
13. McDonald's® and Nike® are two of my sponsors.
14. I am female and 5'10" tall.
15. I'm allergic to peanuts. Are you?
16. I co-wrote a book called *Serving From The Hip: 10 Rules for Living, Loving, and Winning.*
17. Sometimes I compete against my sister.
18. In 2003, I won Wimbledon for the second year in a row.
19. I turned pro at 14.
20. My fashion line, Aneres, is my name spelled backwards.

3

People

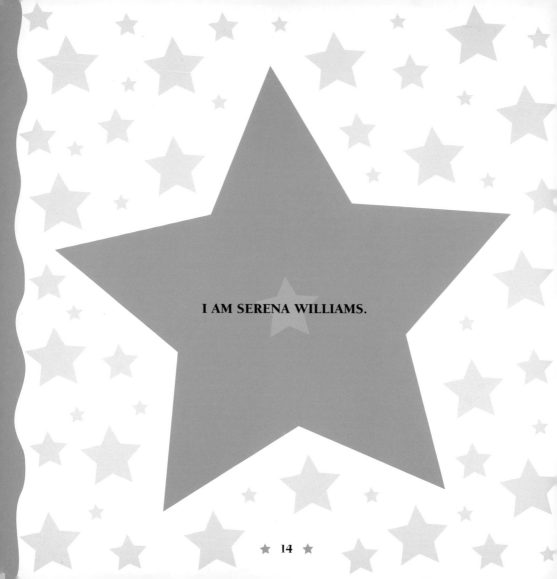

I AM SERENA WILLIAMS.

for girls

I am a Person

1. I share my name with a town in Florida.
2. If I were a girl, I'd be a real drama queen.
3. If you're American, I might sound different to you.
4. I'm an actor.
5. I take my work very seriously.
6. You may not know it, but I've struggled with dyslexia.
7. I've won a Teen Choice Award or two.
8. I was born in England.
9. Girls around the globe are charmed by my good looks.
10. I trained at the British American Drama Academy.
11. In 2002, *Teen People* named me one of its 25 Hottest Stars under 25.
12. You might have seen me in the Caribbean.
13. My Rings are not something you put on your finger.
14. I was forced to wear pointy ears for a long period of time.
15. Kate has been my date.
16. My elves have nothing to do with the North Pole.
17. I played Will Turner.
18. My first name starts and ends with O.
19. I've worked with Brad Pitt and Johnny Depp.
20. I'm not a flower, but I am a Bloom.

People

I AM ORLANDO BLOOM.

I am a Person

1. I am not American.
2. I am rich.
3. I am female.
4. You could say I'm quite a character.
5. I demand a lot from my dad.
6. I won an important contest, but I had a lot of help.
7. In England, my name means wart. Gross!
8. You may have read about me.
9. I've been featured in two hit movies.
10. Some factory workers wrote and sang a song about me.
11. I'm either a bad egg or a bad nut, depending on the story.
12. I'm one of five very lucky kids.
13. My bratty attitude made me lose a golden opportunity.
14. I got thrown down a garbage chute.
15. Roald Dahl created me.
16. Tim Burton brought me back to life on the big screen in 2005.
17. I've decided I don't really like squirrels so much after all.
18. I know Charlie, Violet, Mike and Augustus.
19. I prefer Salt to pepper.
20. I got a golden ticket.

People

I AM VERUCA SALT.

20 Questions for girls

I am a Person

1. I wear red, white and blue but I am not a flag.
2. I am *not* male.
3. I am a Prince in disguise.
4. I wear my crown without a gown.
5. I'm not a comedian, but I did start out as a comic.
6. I often save my boyfriend from certain doom.
7. My jewelry has multiple uses.
8. Giganta, Cheetah, Dr. Poison and Hypnota are some of my enemies.
9. I am a powerful role model for young girls.
10. I was the star of a 1970s TV show.
11. I'm never without my lasso, but I'm not a cowboy.
12. I made Lynda Carter famous.
13. According to some, I grew up on Paradise Isle.
14. I have special bracelets.
15. My jet is hard to see.
16. I have superpowers but no cape.
17. My movie is scheduled to hit theaters in 2007.
18. I started doing my thing during World War II.
19. I am a member of the Justice League.
20. D.C. Comics made me famous.

People

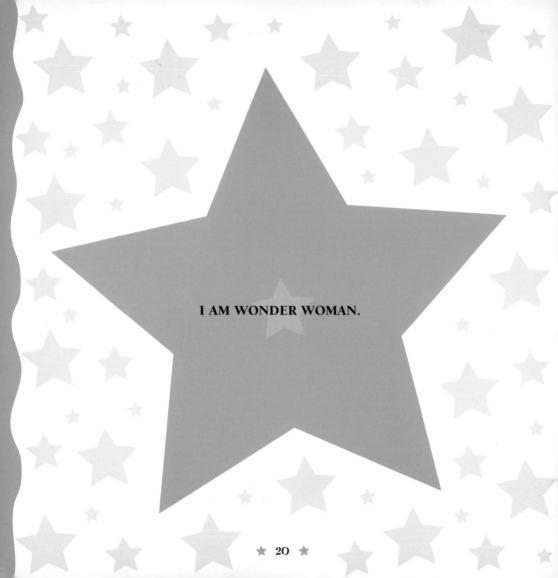

I AM WONDER WOMAN.

I am a Person

1. I am a living female.
2. I was born in Houston, TX on September 28, 1987.
3. I am an actress and a singer.
4. I am a spokesperson for Kids With a Cause.
5. I put out a collection of Christmas songs called *Santa Claus Lane*.
6. You can catch me on TV and at the movies.
7. I've worked for Disney but I've never been on *The Mickey Mouse Club*.
8. I performed as a ballerina when I was six.
9. I had a #1 single but it's like, "So Yesterday."
10. I co-starred in the movie *Agent Cody Banks*.
11. My band members' nicknames are Rone-Shoelaces, Fiver, Baby, Walker and Double-Shot.
12. I'm not Cinderella but I know her story.
13. Ashton Kutcher and I were both in the movie *Cheaper by the Dozen*.
14. I know Joel from Good Charlotte.
15. In 2005, I released my third album, *Most Wanted*.
16. Due to my popularity, I've been called a Tween Queen.
17. My older sister Haylie is also a musician.
18. My accessories line, Stuff, rhymes with my last name.
19. You've probably seen my character Lizzie McGuire on TV and at the movies.
20. I hosted the 2005 Teen Choice Awards with Rob Schneider.

People

I AM A HILARY DUFF.

I am a Person

1. I am part of an American institution.
2. I am female.
3. I can be found in over 80 countries.
4. My members wear uniforms.
5. I believe in girl power!
6. My favorite flower is a Daisy.
7. Once I learn how to fix a leaky toilet, you can call me Ms. Fix-It.
8. My favorite color is green.
9. I am between 5 and 17 years old.
10. You must earn your wings and "fly up" to become one of me.
11. My members have summer camps.
12. I am famous for my thin mints.
13. I have been around for 70 years.
14. I believe in following the leader.
15. Good deeds earn badges for me.
16. I have a special handshake.
17. I am known for selling cookies.
18. My motto is "Be prepared."
19. I love Brownies.
20. A group of me is called a troop.

People

I AM A GIRL SCOUT.

I am a Person

1. I have long, skinny legs.
2. I live in a barn.
3. I talk to chickens.
4. My web has nothing to do with the Internet.
5. I have many children.
6. I am very smart.
7. I saved the life of a friend.
8. I travel to fairs.
9. I have a book named after me.
10. I collect insects.
11. I was born in 1952.
12. I make silk.
13. Farm animals look up to me.
14. If you were a scientist, you would call me *araneus cavaticus*.
15. I am female.
16. I know a rat named Templeton.
17. E.B. White created me.
18. In my 2006 movie, Julia Roberts gives me a voice.
19. I write messages.
20. I think Wilbur is "Some Pig."

9

People

**I AM CHARLOTTE
(FROM *CHARLOTTE'S WEB*).**

I am a Person

1. I was born in 1972.
2. I'm a real team player.
3. A lot of girls see me as a role model.
4. I like to assist my co-workers whenever I can.
5. I'm very goal-oriented.
6. I'm not a photographer, but I do like to shoot.
7. *People* magazine once put me on their 50 Most Beautiful People in the World list.
8. I get a real kick out of my job.
9. I have fancy footwork.
10. I retired in 2004 at the age of 32.
11. Having a ball is very important to me.
12. I am an athlete.
13. I played for the University of North Carolina.
14. ESPN awarded me Female Athlete of the Year, twice.
15. I've won two Olympic gold medals.
16. I know Brandi, Kristine and Michelle.
17. At 19, I was the youngest American woman in my sport to be in a World Cup championship.
18. I am not a show-off, but I am a Hamm.
19. I play soccer.
20. I was born Mariel Margaret, but people call me Mia.

10

People

I AM MIA HAMM.

I am a Person

1. I was born in 1978.
2. I have a twin brother.
3. I grew up in Iowa.
4. I've used a hidden camera, but I'm not a spy.
5. I started as a Calvin Klein model.
6. I make celebrities nervous.
7. I am an actor.
8. In 2002, *Teen People* named me one of its 25 Hottest Stars under 25.
9. I got kicked out of a play in high school.
10. Before I got discovered, I was studying to be a biochemical engineer.
11. Two of my left toes are fused together. Creepy!
12. I date Demi.
13. Rumer, Scout and Tallulah Belle call me MOD.
14. Wilmer and P. Diddy are friends of mine.
15. One of my favorite questions is *Dude, Where's My Car?*
16. You might have seen me on *That '70s Show*.
17. I know things are *Cheaper By the Dozen.*
18. I have a show on MTV.
19. My initials are A.K.
20. I might Punk you.

People

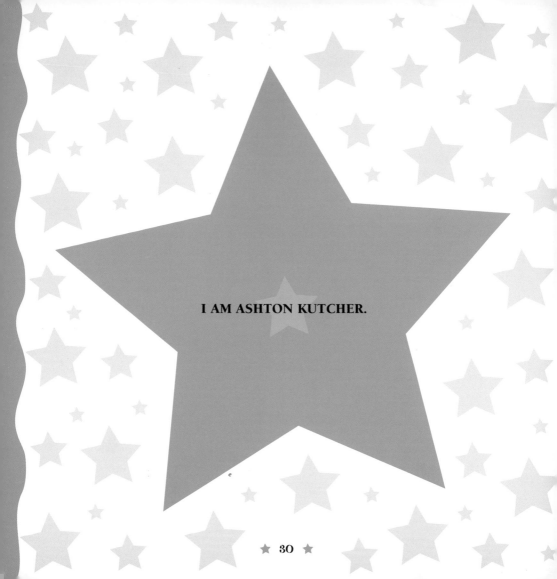

I AM ASHTON KUTCHER.

I am a Person

1. I'm not a dork, but I am a square.
2. I can hold my breath for a really long time.
3. My favorite color is yellow. What's yours?
4. You can find me at the mall, the movies, the bookstore—lots of places!
5. I have a goofy bucked-tooth grin.
6. I get very excited about things!!!
7. I don't work in an office, but I do wear a tie.
8. My favorite hobbies are karate and jellyfishing.
9. I am a celebrated cook
10. I love pineapple.
11. My best friend's name is Patrick.
12. I've been voted Employee of the Month almost 400 times.
13. My legs are seaworthy.
14. Pants are very important to me.
15. Both my first and last names have two syllables.
16. My sponge has nothing to do with cleaning.
17. I am a cartoon character.
18. I live in Bikini Bottom.
19. "I'm ready, I'm ready, I'm ready-eady-eady-eady-eady-eady-eady!"
20. My initials are S.S.

12

People

I AM SPONGEBOB SQUAREPANTS®.

I am a Person

1. I'm very competitive.
2. My parents moved from China to the US before I was born.
3. I wear pretty dresses to work.
4. I turned 25 in 2005.
5. My motto is "Work hard, have fun and be yourself."
6. I've had a lot of coaching.
7. My routine is never dull.
8. I always wear a good luck necklace, given to me by my grandmother.
9. I have fans all around the world.
10. People expect me to retire young.
11. I can spin circles around you.
12. I've been called a "jumping bean."
13. My boots aren't a fashion statement.
14. To me, practice makes perfect.
15. Being graceful is part of my job.
16. As of 2005, I have two Olympic Medals.
17. I've got a great figure eight.
18. I'm not lazy, but I do like to skate by.
19. Some people think I'm an ice princess.
20. My last name rhymes with swan.

13

People

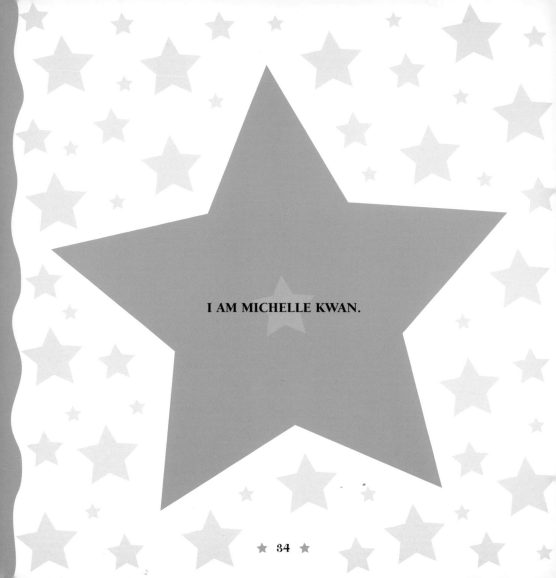

I AM MICHELLE KWAN.

I am a Person

1. I was born in Kansas.
2. I got lost somewhere between New Guinea and Howland Island.
3. I am female.
4. I had a very adventurous spirit.
5. People were—and still are—fascinated by me.
6. I learned to fly in California.
7. I was the first woman to fly over the Atlantic as a passenger.
8. I attended Columbia University.
9. I disappeared mysteriously in 1937.
10. I loved to fly but I did not have wings.
11. I once worked as a nurse.
12. I saw my first airplane when I was 10 years old.
13. I first flew over the Atlantic in 1928.
14. I tried to fly around the world.
15. Some say I may have been taken captive.
16. Hundreds of books have been written about me.
17. I married George Palmer Putnam.
18. I am a pilot.
19. My initials are A.E.
20. My last name is not Bedelia.

14

People

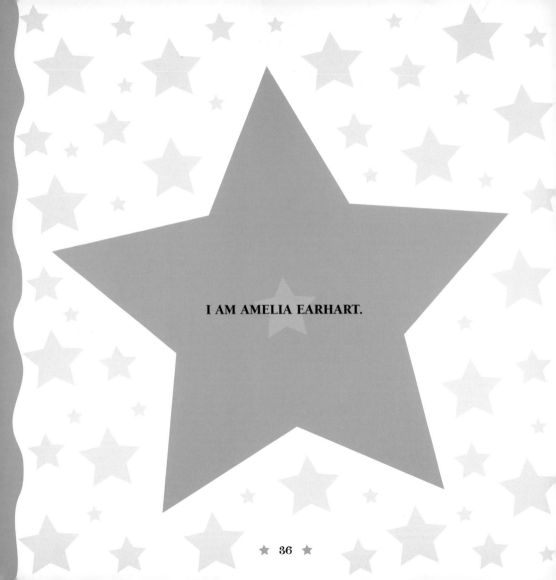

I AM AMELIA EARHART.

I am a Person

1. I am a female.
2. My creator was a mathematician.
3. I almost lost my head.
4. I am British.
5. I've enjoyed tea parties.
6. I don't know if I mean what I say or I say what I mean.
7. I fell down a hole.
8. I had an unusual adventure.
9. I've known some real cards.
10. I visited another world.
11. I've celebrated un-birthdays.
12. I was involved in a famous trial.
13. I have gone through the looking glass.
14. I am fictional.
15. My height bothers me.
16. My favorite outfit is a blue dress and a white pinafore.
17. I have a friend whose smile stays with me.
18. I've been to the movies and in books.
19. I know someone who is late for dates.
20. I traveled through Wonderland.

15

People

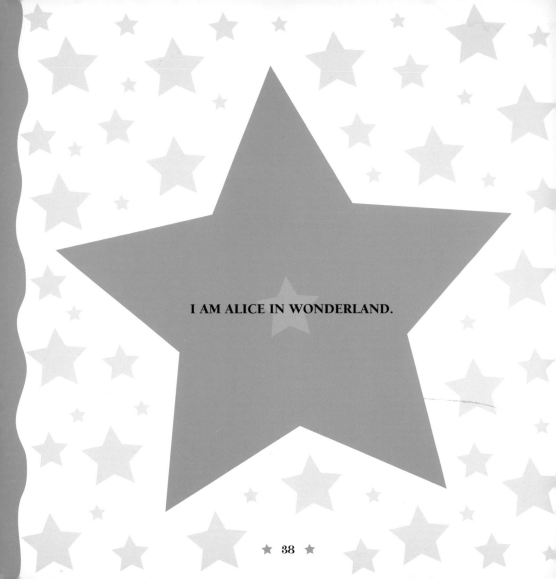

I AM ALICE IN WONDERLAND.

I am a Person

1. I died in 1968.
2. I am a female.
3. I am famous for my tremendous will power.
4. A mini-musical version of my life was featured in *South Park*.
5. Alexander Graham Bell helped me find a teacher.
6. I spent my life lecturing to benefit the physically challenged.
7. I graduated from Radcliffe College.
8. I made history when I graduated from college in 1904.
9. I inspired the award-winning play and movie *The Miracle Worker*.
10. I came into the world perfectly healthy.
11. My first famous words were "wah-wah" for water.
12. I wrote *The Story of My Life*.
13. I suffered from "acute congestion."
14. I come from Alabama.
15. When I was young, I screamed and threw terrible tantrums.
16. I have the same first name as the beautiful woman from Troy.
17. I became blind and deaf at age two.
18. I learned to read English, French, German, Greek and Latin in Braille.
19. I spelled out words in people's palms.
20. Anne Sullivan was my teacher.

16

People

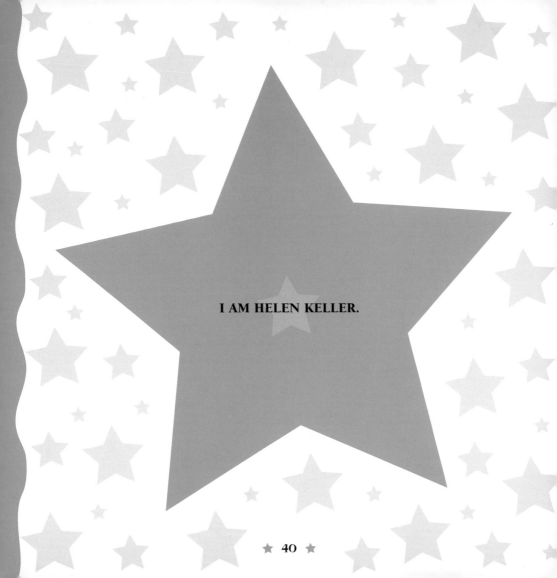

I AM HELEN KELLER.

I am a Person

1. I'm very animated.
2. I am the hero of a book.
3. My life story has made people cry.
4. I live in the forest.
5. I walk on four legs.
6. I am not real.
7. I am an animal.
8. My mother was dear to me.
9. My father is very fast.
10. The person who invented me was Felix Salten.
11. I have a friend who's a musical rabbit.
12. I came to the world in the middle of a thicket.
13. I came into being in 1926.
14. Faline is my sweetheart.
15. I had spots in my youth.
16. Man is my enemy.
17. The animals of the forest speak to me.
18. One of my friends is Ronno.
19. In 1942, I reached the movie theaters.
20. Flower is the name of my favorite skunk.

17

People

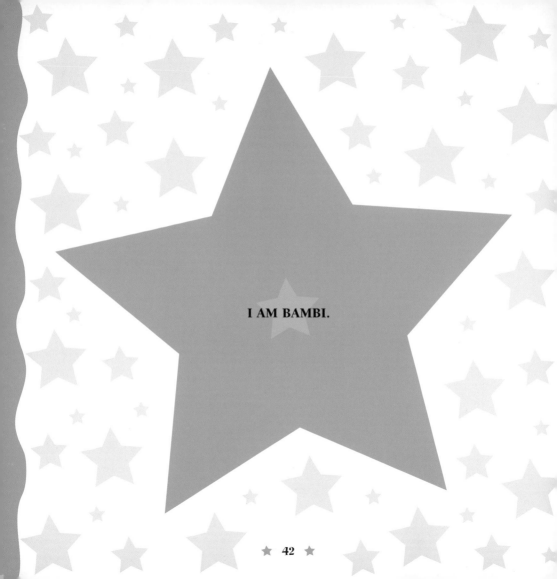

I AM BAMBI.

I am a Person

1. I'm OK with reality.
2. I was born in Texas in 1984.
3. At 11, I was the youngest person ever admitted to the School of American Ballet.
4. My fans keep me cool.
5. *Entertainment Weekly* named me Breakout Star of 2004.
6. In show business, I'm what is called a triple threat.
7. I was nominated for four 2005 Teen Choice Awards.
8. I hang with the young Hollywood in-crowd.
9. I got *Punk'd* in 2005.
10. My first album went to #1.
11. I had my own show on MTV.
12. I'm not an angel, but I did make it to *7th Heaven.*
13. My dad used to be a preacher, but now he's my manager.
14. I'm not ditzy, but I do live in "La La" land.
15. I dated Ryan.
16. My *Autobiography* was a huge success.
17. I've been in my older sister's shadow.
18. Lip-synching is a very sore subject with me.
19. I'm happy to share "Pieces of Me."
20. I am not a cartoon character, but I am a Simpson.

18

People

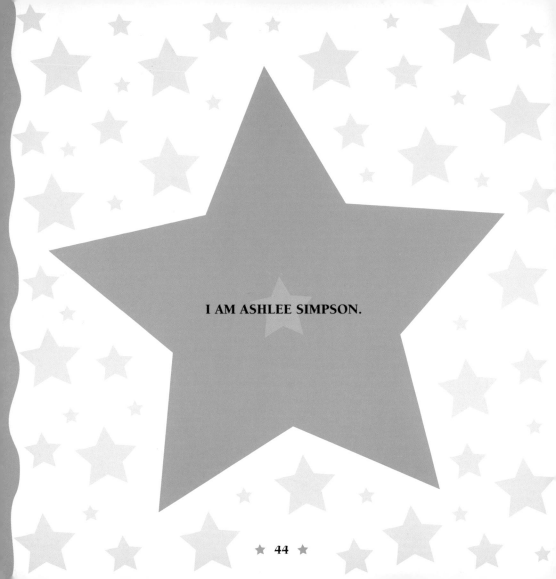

I AM ASHLEE SIMPSON.

I am a Person

1. I do all of the cleaning at home.
2. I am female.
3. Next party I attend, I'm taking a watch.
4. My life is a real fairy tale.
5. My glassware is not intended for drinking.
6. Mice have been nice to me.
7. My curfew is midnight.
8. I am known only by my first name.
9. My wardrobe is in need of serious help.
10. My slippers are not warm and fuzzy.
11. My godmother is very creative with pumpkins.
12. My ball is not round.
13. I say, "If the shoe fits, wear it."
14. I am fictional.
15. Someday my prince will come.
16. My step-sisters have big feet.
17. Drew Barrymore put a new spin on my tale in *Ever After*.
18. My stepmother and I don't really get along.
19. Walt Disney brought my character to the big screen.
20. Hilary Duff knows my story.

19

People

I AM CINDERELLA.

I am a Person

1. I am not American.
2. I was born in 1970.
3. I can swing a stick.
4. I'm not a party girl, but I do love to go clubbing.
5. I've broken a few records.
6. I started playing a round at 12 years old.
7. In college, I was still an amateur.
8. Now, I'm a pro.
9. I'm not the jealous type, but I do see green a lot.
10. I've pocketed a lot of prize money.
11. Sometimes I drive a cart to work.
12. A certain letter in my name might löök ödd to yöu.
13. I joined the women's circuit in 1993.
14. I like to putt around.
15. I love the smell of fresh-cut grass.
16. I think sand can be the pits.
17. I am tee-rific at what I do.
18. My favorite number is fore!
19. I am not a meatball, but I am Swedish.
20. I am a famous golfer.

People

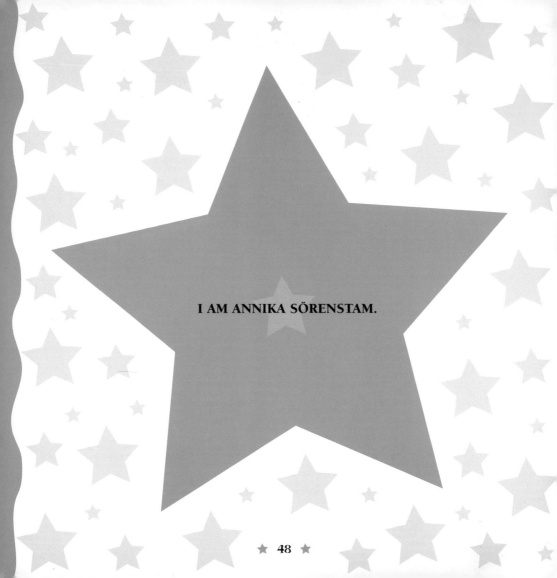

I AM ANNIKA SÖRENSTAM.

I am a Person

1. I come from a good family.
2. I get my picture taken a lot.
3. I was born on June 21, 1982.
4. My mother died tragically young.
5. I am very posh.
6. Yanks think I have an accent.
7. I cannot fly in the same plane with my dad.
8. My grandmother is Elizabeth.
9. I am not Billy and my Dad is not Chuck.
10. I've been called "The Royal Dreamboat."
11. My crown isn't on my tooth.
12. My full name is William Arthur Philip Louis.
13. People put HRH in front of my name.
14. I am a real Prince, not the fairy tale kind.
15. I chose St. Andrew's College.
16. Ick! My job starts when my grandma and my dad die.
17. Harry is my little brother.
18. My dad is the Prince of Wales.
19. My mom was named Diana.
20. I will probably be King.

21

People

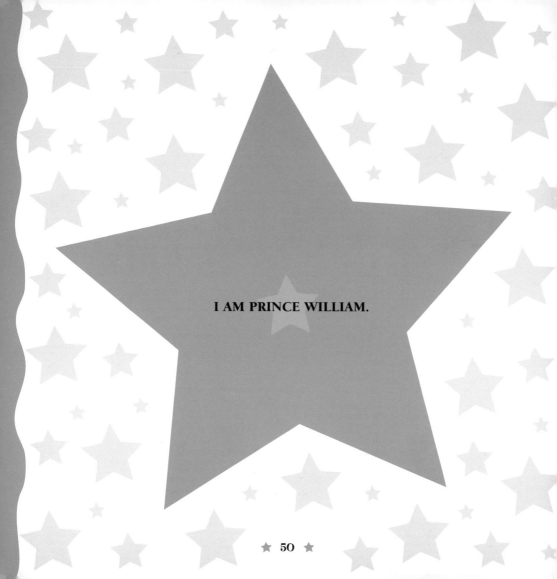

I AM PRINCE WILLIAM.

I am a Person

1. You may have learned about me in class.
2. My story is legendary.
3. I died very young.
4. I am female.
5. I am a native American Indian.
6. There is a national park named after me.
7. My father was a chief.
8. I saved the life of a captain.
9. I am a princess.
10. Disney made a movie about me.
11. I helped negotiate peace.
12. My tribe hails from Virginia.
13. I was kidnapped.
14. Legend has it that I was born sometime in the late 1600s.
15. My hair falls to my waist.
16. I was born in the New World.
17. My name was changed to Rebecca Rolfe after I got married.
18. John Smith was close to my heart.
19. I was brought to England to meet King James and his court.
20. Most people know me by my nickname, which means "playful girl" in Powhatan.

22

People

I AM POCAHONTAS.

I am a Person

1. I turned 20 in 2005.
2. I was born in Atlanta, GA.
3. I am an American girl.
4. Now, I'm an actress and a singer.
5. My name might remind you of a bird.
6. I've won the Nickelodeon Kids' Choice Award for Favorite TV Actress more than once.
7. I have my own fragrance and clothing line, among other things.
8. My Cheetah has no spots.
9. I love cheese grits with shrimp. Yum!
10. Some people think I'm psychic.
11. I starred on *The Cosby Show* back in the day.
12. I can't talk to the animals, but I have worked with Dr. Dolittle—twice.
13. I got *Punk'd* in 2005.
14. I've played a princess, but I won't let you read my diary.
15. I know "That's What Little Girls Are Made Of."
16. I think Kim is Possible.
17. I've spent some time *Hangin' with Mr. Cooper*.
18. I'm big on the Disney Channel.
19. My initials are R.S.
20. When I was a little kid, I signed with the Ford Modeling Agency.

23

People

I AM RAVEN-SYMONE.

I am a Person

1. I have a British accent.
2. I believe in experiencing art.
3. I am female.
4. P.L. Travers wrote a series of books about me.
5. Jane and Michael are my charges.
6. I am fictional.
7. I am known to pop in and pop out.
8. My film won five Academy Awards® in 1964, including Best Actress and Best Song.
9. I worked for the Banks, but I know nothing of investments.
10. My carpetbag is much bigger than it looks.
11. I worked at Number 17 Cherry Tree Lane.
12. I tend to leave when the wind changes.
13. I enjoy flying kites.
14. Walt Disney made a movie about me.
15. I advocate taking medication with sugar.
16. Some have called me "Nanny."
17. I have a good friend who is a chimney sweep.
18. I always travel with an umbrella.
19. Julie Andrews played me in a movie.
20. Supercalifragilisticexpialidocious!

24

People

I AM MARY POPPINS.

Places

I am a Place

1. Central Park is found in me.
2. I am a city.
3. The Statue of Liberty can see me.
4. I am American.
5. My garden on Madison Square is no bed of roses.
6. My old name was New Amsterdam.
7. If you've been on Broadway, you've been to me.
8. I have the Brooklyn Bridge.
9. My Yankees never fought in the Civil War.
10. The subway is my favorite transportation.
11. I am home to the United Nations.
12. I have Queens, but no kings.
13. I was once my country's capital.
14. I house the Empire State Building.
15. Many of my streets are numbered.
16. My Jets fly in New Jersey.
17. My cabs are yellow.
18. I have Grand Central Station.
19. Immigrants came to my Ellis Island.
20. They call me the Big Apple.

Places

I AM NEW YORK CITY.

I am a Place

1. I am American.
2. I am neither a state nor a city.
3. My winters are never white.
4. You can't compare me to an apple.
5. Some people think I'm superficial.
6. I have lots of palm trees.
7. My state is Golden.
8. I'm not as smoggy as L.A.
9. I have a large Latino population.
10. South Coast Plaza is my main mall.
11. I border the Pacific Ocean.
12. Come to me to get a tan.
13. I house the Ronald Reagan Library.
14. Some parts of me are very expensive.
15. Visit Disneyland and you visit me.
16. Gwen Stefani grew up in me.
17. I'm home to Laguna Beach.
18. A TV show made me famous.
19. A lot of people call me by my initials.
20. Seth, Ryan, Marisa and Summer live in me.

2

Places

I AM ORANGE COUNTY, CA
(THE O.C.).

I am a Place

1. At noon in New York, my sun is just rising.
2. My alphabet has only 12 letters.
3. I was formed by volcanoes.
4. I was originally called the Sandwich Islands.
5. I call the continental US "The Mainland."
6. My spicy raw tuna is called poki.
7. I contain 132 islands, reefs and shoals.
8. I am a favorite vacation spot.
9. My people tell stories with their hands.
10. My natives are called Polynesians.
11. My beaches are world famous.
12. I have necklaces made out of flowers.
13. I am the 50th state
14. I might greet you with an aloha.
15. I am home to sugar cane, pineapples and macadamia nuts.
16. The Pacific is my ocean.
17. My people hula without hoops.
18. I was featured in the surfing movie *Blue Crush*.
19. Visit me and you might attend a luau.
20. My most famous beach is Waikiki.

3

Places

I AM HAWAII.

I am a Place

1. My country has its own sea.
2. I am home to over 12 million people!
3. My heart is the Imperial Palace.
4. A long time ago, my kids celebrated their birthdays on January 1st, instead of on their real birthday.
5. I have shrines, temples and castles.
6. I have my own Disneyland.
7. I am not American.
8. My country's flag has a red circle on it, which stands for the Sun.
9. My noodles are called soba and udon.
10. The Ginza District can be found inside me.
11. I don't have dollars, but I do have yen.
12. I am famous for my pretty pinkish-white cherry blossoms.
13. I am on an island.
14. My kids are known for their fashion sense.
15. I celebrate Hina Matsuri, which means the Doll's Festival (or Girl's Festival), on March 3rd.
16. My alphabet has characters, not letters.
17. I love sushi!
18. My people drink sake.
19. My cartoons are called animé.
20. I am the capital city of Japan.

4

Places

I AM TOKYO.

I am a Place

1. White is my favorite color.
2. My name starts and ends with the same letter.
3. I have giant mountain ranges.
4. Admiral Byrd explored me.
5. I have no native people.
6. I am the least populated of my kind.
7. There are no trees or plants on me.
8. I have very long winters.
9. I'm not a very popular vacation spot.
10. I have whales and seals.
11. I am south of almost everything.
12. For six straight months, I never see the sun.
13. I have lots of ice.
14. I am a continent.
15. I am the coldest place on Earth.
16. I have an icy coastline.
17. My first three letters spell the name of an insect.
18. I'm featured in *March of the Penguins*.
19. I have icebergs and glaciers.
20. I cover the South Pole.

5

Places

I AM ANTARCTICA.

I am a Place

1. I'm hard to see when I'm new.
2. I am not made of green cheese.
3. It's easy to see me at night.
4. I orbit around Earth.
5. I fly an American flag.
6. Humans first visited me by spaceship in 1969.
7. I am smaller than the Earth.
8. You can see me from anywhere.
9. Neil Armstrong was the first person to visit me.
10. People talk about the man in me.
11. One side of me is always dark.
12. Wolves like to howl at me.
13. Some are superstitious about me when I am full.
14. I am in the sky.
15. I am as old as Earth.
16. A cow jumped over me in a nursery rhyme.
17. I reflect light from the sun.
18. I'm yellow in Lucky Charms™ cereal.
19. My pull affects the ocean's tides.
20. I can go from quarter to half to full without changing size.

6

Places

I AM THE MOON.

I am a Place

1. I am located north of the equator.
2. I am American.
3. I am home to many stars, but no planets.
4. You may see me in the movies.
5. Most people think I'm glamorous.
6. Sunset and Vine are my streets.
7. I am a city.
8. I am not on the East Coast.
9. My name suggests that I am a type of timber.
10. My fame started in the Twentieth Century.
11. My name is on a hill.
12. I can see the Pacific Ocean.
13. Many visit me to catch a rising star.
14. I am the world's movie capital.
15. My name lights up at night.
16. A lot of movie stars live in my hills.
17. There are lots of songs about me.
18. I am found in California.
19. My Chinese Theatre is a popular place to visit.
20. I have a sidewalk with stars on it.

Places

I AM HOLLYWOOD.

I am a Place

1. I was born in 1971.
2. I am home to Liberty Square.
3. I am twice the size of New York City.
4. I have a castle, but I am not ruled by a king.
5. You will see lots of animals if you visit me.
6. I am in the US.
7. I'm located on 43 square miles of former swampland.
8. I am one of the happiest places on earth.
9. I saw 10 million people in 1971.
10. My creator never saw me.
11. I am in the Sunshine State.
12. Every night I light up the sky.
13. You may go head over heels when you visit me.
14. I've got mice that aren't afraid of cats.
15. You can see Pluto when you visit me.
16. My entire town shuts down and is thoroughly cleaned every single night.
17. Las Vegas is the only place with more hotels than me.
18. I love to be visited by kids of all ages.
19. I am one of the most visited tourist attractions in the world.
20. I've got land in California.

Places

I AM WALT DISNEY WORLD.

I am a Place

1. I am in America.
2. I am not a city or a state.
3. I am named for a US president.
4. Maryland and Virginia donated land to me.
5. I am very political.
6. The Potomac River flows by me.
7. I'm home to the Smithsonian Institute.
8. I have a very famous Monument.
9. I house America's largest library.
10. You can see me on TV.
11. I am a tourist attraction.
12. Every year I host the Cherry Blossom Festival.
13. Congress makes my laws
14. The Supreme Court meets in me.
15. I am home to Capitol Hill.
16. I can see the Lincoln Memorial.
17. My House is White.
18. My zoo is famous for its pandas.
19. I am the nation's capital.
20. My initials stand for District of Columbia.

Places

I AM WASHINGTON, D.C.

I am a Place

1. People watch—and listen—to me.
2. I'm a place of business.
3. I first got started before you were born, way back in 1981.
4. My cables won't start cars.
5. My name is always abbreviated.
6. I am in a major US city.
7. My lights are bright.
8. People come to me to promote their work.
9. Fans hang out beneath my windows.
10. I helped make Britney and Beyoncé such familiar faces.
11. I am in a Square.
12. I like to countdown to the top.
13. I'll get you in to some *Super Sweet 16* parties.
14. I can't drive, but I do observe *Road Rules*.
15. Music is very important to me.
16. I'm part of the *Real World*.
17. I host my own video and movie awards.
18. My network also owns Nickelodeon.
19. I host *TRL*.
20. I am a TV studio.

10

Places

I AM MTV STUDIOS
(IN TIMES SQUARE).

♥ 78 ♥

I am a Place

1. I am a country.
2. My queen was nicknamed "Bloody Mary."
3. My money is measured in pounds.
4. I'm not a TV, but I do have a Channel.
5. I am in Europe.
6. I first made the mini-skirt popular.
7. My people call cookies "biscuits."
8. I give birth to a lot of great bands.
9. America was once my colony.
10. If you play my football, you'll use your feet.
11. J.K. Rowling was born in me.
12. I am the largest country in the United Kingdom.
13. Madonna lives on one of my estates.
14. My people call elevators "lifts."
15. Teatime is one of my traditions.
16. I have red double-decker buses.
17. London is my capital.
18. I'm part of an island.
19. I'm famous for my fish and chips.
20. Princes William and Harry call me home.

11

Places

I AM ENGLAND.

I am a Place

1. John Wesley Powell gave me my name.
2. I've got a river running through me.
3. The Colorado River made me.
4. I am in America.
5. I'm popular with families.
6. Copper was found in my rocks.
7. I am called "The Spectacular Valley."
8. I am known for my natural beauty.
9. I expose layers of rock.
10. I see three million visitors a year.
11. You can ride a mule to get to the bottom of me.
12. I am considered to be one of earth's great natural wonders.
13. I began six million years ago.
14. I'm a deep valley with steep sides.
15. My rocks are two billion years old.
16. A river eroding layers of rock formed me.
17. I am a favorite hiking area.
18. I became a national park in 1919.
19. *The Brady Bunch* vacationed in me.
20. You'll find me in Arizona.

12

Places

I AM THE GRAND CANYON.

20 Questions for girls

I am a Place

1. There is a famous movie about me.
2. I'm not in the US.
3. I've been written about in many different languages.
4. I am an imaginary place.
5. I'm home to a well-known wizard, but I'm not Hogwarts.
6. I have a famous field of poppies.
7. Munchkinland is one of my counties.
8. I'm known for my slippers.
9. I have an Emerald City.
10. My witches aren't all bad.
11. Frank L. Baum wrote books about me.
12. I have monkeys that fly, but I'm not in the jungle.
13. My ruler rarely comes out from behind his curtain.
14. My lion isn't very brave.
15. I know Toto.
16. I'm very far from Kansas.
17. My scarecrow can speak.
18. My Dorothy thinks, *There's no place like home*.
19. I was filmed in Technicolor.
20. You can find me at the end of the Yellow Brick Road.

13

Places

I AM THE LAND OF OZ.

I am a Place

1. I am a national park.
2. I get my name from high yellow cliffs you can see in me.
3. I'm one of the first of my kind.
4. I have geysers and hot springs.
5. I'm great for hiking and camping.
6. Over two-million people visit me yearly.
7. Part of me is in Wyoming.
8. I am America's largest wildlife preserve.
9. I have bears, elk and bison.
10. I am covered with snow all winter.
11. I am partly in Montana.
12. I came with the Louisiana Purchase.
13. Eagle Peak is my highest point.
14. I have waterfalls and meadows.
15. I have 1000 miles of trails.
16. 80% of me is forest.
17. I have a Grand Canyon.
18. Theodore Roosevelt helped protect me.
19. Come to me to see Old Faithful.
20. You can visit Fort Yellowstone in me.

14

Places

I AM YELLOWSTONE NATIONAL PARK.

I am a Place

1. My population is 3.5 million people.
2. My north is warmer than my south.
3. I have no snakes.
4. I celebrate the signing of the treaty of Waitangi on February 14.
5. I farm perna canaliculas at my Marlborough Sound.
6. The Maori are my native people.
7. Rugby, cricket and soccer are some of my favorite sports.
8. I am a great surfing spot.
9. I call an undershirt a singlet and a washcloth a flannel.
10. Eighty-million sheep inhabit my land.
11. The brave girl Paikea in *Whale Rider* calls me home.
12. My accent sounds British but I'm not from Britain.
13. I have two main islands.
14. My highest mountain is Mt. Cook.
15. My capital is Wellington.
16. I'm known for my Kiwis.
17. Zena, Warrior Princess comes from me.
18. Many associate me with Australia.
19. *The Lord of the Rings* movies were filmed in me.
20. My initials are N.Z.

Places

I AM NEW ZEALAND.

I am a Place

1. I am bigger than a breadbox.
2. My flag is red, white and blue but I'm not American.
3. I attract visitors from all around the world.
4. I don't have a subway, but I do have a metro.
5. Sometimes my people are called frogs.
6. I'm home to the Louvre Museum.
7. I'm European.
8. I'm known for my chic fashion.
9. I inspired a hotel in Las Vegas.
10. The Rugrats visited me in a movie.
11. I am very romantic.
12. My nickname is The City of Light.
13. My river is the Seine.
14. My baguettes are the best.
15. Bonjour!
16. The Eiffel Tower is a famous landmark of mine.
17. My people wear berets.
18. I share my name with one of the Hilton sisters.
19. Madeline calls me home.
20. I'm the capital of France.

16

Places

I AM PARIS.

I am a Place

1. I resemble a marble.
2. Geologists study my make-up.
3. Rearrange my letters and they spell "heart."
4. I have a crust, but I'm not a pie.
5. I'm always moving.
6. When I'm not proper, I'm dirt.
7. My inside is made of hot rocks.
8. People used to think that I was flat.
9. Every time I spin around, a day passes.
10. I am afraid of losing my ozone layers.
11. Dinosaurs used to live on me.
12. I travel around the Sun.
13. About 70% of me is water.
14. I have one moon.
15. How I was created is still up for debate.
16. I am at least 4.5 billion years old.
17. I weigh 6000 billion tons.
18. I am the third planet from the Sun.
19. I have seven continents.
20. I have my own "Day," celebrated every April.

Places

I AM EARTH.

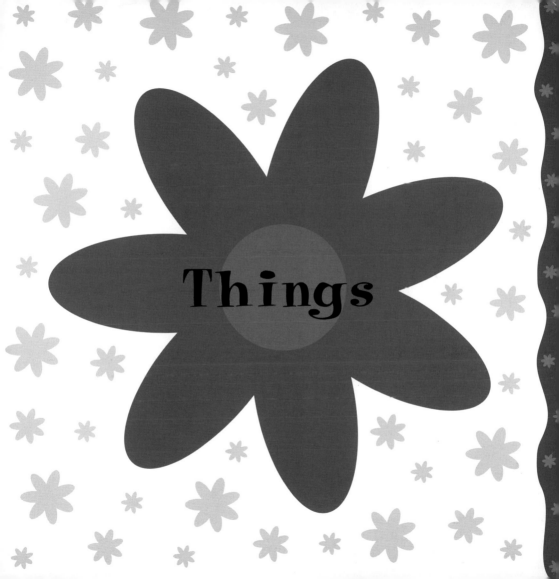

Things

I am a Thing

1. I have a way of making people open up to me.
2. Trust me. I can keep a secret.
3. People might come snooping for me.
4. I'm not all that organized, but I do keep track of things.
5. Believe me, I know how you feel.
6. Some people use me every day, others never use me.
7. I might make you draw a blank, or just doodle.
8. I'm more private than public.
9. I am very Dear to some.
10. I am a five-letter word.
11. Some people keep me under their pillow.
12. Your mom and dad have no business bothering me
13. I know a lot about you.
14. I sometimes come with a lock.
15. I'm not nosy, but I am full of juicy gossip.
16. I might embarrass you if I got into the wrong hands.
17. I help you express yourself.
18. Boys might call me a journal.
19. Online, I'm called a blog.
20. Anne Frank kept me.

Things

I AM A DIARY.

I am a Thing

1. I come from the East.
2. I might make you sweat.
3. I'm not a door but I do need a mat.
4. I have my own pants.
5. I need your body to do my thing.
6. I am a four-letter word that can be a noun.
7. You can learn about me from a teacher.
8. Some people find me relaxing.
9. I'll make you stretch your limits.
10. I do a body good.
11. I like to meditate.
12. I am believed to be about 6,000 years old.
13. People practice me, and then keep practicing me.
14. I started in India, but most of the world likes me.
15. I take about ninety minutes to fully experience.
16. My lotus is not a flower.
17. Iyengar and Bikram are two of my styles.
18. I require flexibility.
19. I rhyme with toga.
20. I'll make you strike a pose—and hold it.

Things

I AM YOGA.

I am a Thing

1. I need a computer to do my job.
2. I'm a seasoned traveler
3. I'm not a singer, but I can carry a tune.
4. I'm very trim.
5. People of all kinds listen to what I have to say.
6. I've never been convicted, but I have been charged.
7. To some, I'm a status symbol.
8. I respond well to a light touch.
9. I'm not a therapist, but I don't mind if you download on me.
10. I'll cost you a pretty penny.
11. I come in mini shapes and sizes.
12. I'm music to your ears.
13. I prefer Apples to oranges.
14. I've never been paid, but I've had lots of Jobs.
15. i ignore a primary rule of grammar.
16. I'm no Casanova, but I am quite a player.
17. White is my signature color.
18. I'm a high-tech gadget.
19. I'm not a pea but I do have a Pod.
20. I'm a new-school version of a Walkman®.

3

Things

I AM AN iPOD®.

✻ 100 ✻

20 Questions for girls

I am a Thing

1. I'm a type of dance.
2. I see lots of legs.
3. I need special shoes.
4. I have different companies.
5. I can be modern or classical.
6. You wear tights to do me.
7. I am carefully choreographed.
8. I am very graceful.
9. My movements are precise.
10. I may tell a story.
11. Kids take lessons tutu learn me.
12. I may have costumes.
13. I made Maria Tallchief and Rudolf Nureyev famous.
14. I need music to do my thing.
15. I require lots of practice and training.
16. You might need a ticket to see me.
17. I'll show you *Romeo and Juliet*.
18. I'm an art form.
19. Some cities have special houses for me.
20. If you've seen *The Nutcracker*, you've seen me.

4

Things

I AM BALLET.

I am a Thing

1. I was invented in 1958.
2. I'm American.
3. Twenty-five million people bought me within four months of my debut.
4. I go right to your waist.
5. Arthur Melin and Richard Knerr invented me.
6. I come in many different designs and colors.
7. I don't wear earrings but I do like hoops.
8. It requires skill to keep me going.
9. I make a sound when I go round.
10. I don't rock, but I can roll.
11. I get tubular, dude.
12. I love to go for a spin.
13. Boys like me too.
14. I'm made of plastic.
15. Some kids use me like a jump rope.
16. Wham-O® owns me.
17. Despite my name, I'm not Hawaiian.
18. I'm not a baton, but I do like to twirl.
19. I'm spelled with a hyphen.
20. I'm a classic summertime toy.

5

Things

I AM A HULA-HOOP®.

I am a Thing

1. I can be hot or cold.
2. I can be white or light.
3. I don't drink, but I show up in bars.
4. Although I'm not wealthy, I am rich.
5. My chips aren't for your computer.
6. My beans aren't found in a burrito.
7. I can come before or after milk.
8. I owe some of my success to the Easter Bunny.
9. Some people say that the Swiss make me best.
10. I am sometimes used in fondue.
11. I come on sundaes.
12. Both girls and boys find me irresistible.
13. I'm not a professor, but if you rearrange me, I "teach cool."
14. Sometimes I'm nutty.
15. I am popular worldwide.
16. Like true love, I can be bittersweet.
17. The Aztec and Mayan Indians knew me first.
18. Although I can be filled, I'm never full.
19. If you've got a sweet tooth, I can satisfy it.
20. Willy Wonka created an entire factory just for me.

6

Things

I AM CHOCOLATE.

I am a Thing

1. I can be long or short.
2. I'm a big investment.
3. I used to made out of wood.
4. I won't yawn, even though I'm board.
5. I'll take you for a ride.
6. I am popular with youngsters and oldsters.
7. I am required equipment in some sport events.
8. You'll find me at the beach.
9. Gidget made me popular in the late 1950s.
10. I'm not a dolphin, but I do have a fin.
11. I like to float.
12. Swell is one of my favorite words.
13. I don't shave, but I do get waxed.
14. You can ding me, but you can't dong me.
15. I get really psyched when I see a set.
16. Some of my biggest advocates go snowboarding in the winter.
17. People stand on me when I'm doing my thing.
18. I'm not from London, but I do love the tube.
19. Sharks have been known to take a bite out of me.
20. Kate Bosworth used me in *Blue Crush*.

Things

I AM A SURFBOARD.

20 Questions for girls

I am a Thing

1. I am an American institution.
2. I'm usually delivered.
3. I help raise money for a good cause.
4. I come in a box.
5. I only come around once a year.
6. I sometimes end up in the freezer.
7. I'm always associated with females.
8. I've seen a lot of milk in my time.
9. Despite me name, I'm made for boys too.
10. You can't find me in supermarkets.
11. My peanut butter doesn't come with jelly.
12. If you know Trefoil, you know me.
13. I'm a dieter's nightmare.
14. My girls wear green.
15. My lemons aren't sour.
16. My girls wear uniforms.
17. I can satisfy your sweet tooth.
18. I'm sold door-to-door.
19. When I'm thin, I'm minty.
20. My providers started as Guides; now they're Scouts.

8

Things

I AM GIRL SCOUT® COOKIES.

I am a Thing

1. Some people care more about me than others.
2. I am very down to earth.
3. I turned 30 in 2000.
4. Green is my favorite color.
5. I encourage people to keep it clean.
6. To me, nothing beats a nice breath of fresh air.
7. I think waste is hazardous.
8. I like to talk trash.
9. I've never been on a bus or subway, but I support public transportation.
10. According to the zodiac, I'm a Taurus.
11. I am a national holiday.
12. I say, if it's yellow let it mellow.
13. Tree huggers love me.
14. People use me to spread a message.
15. I only come round once a year.
16. I'm not lazy, but I try to conserve my energy.
17. If you care about the planet, you care about me.
18. I love to recycle.
19. I'm very aware of my environment.
20. I am celebrated worldwide on April 22nd every year.

Things

I AM EARTH DAY.

I am a Thing

1. I have committed no crime, but I am often charged.
2. I keep getting smaller and smaller.
3. You don't want to eat my chips.
4. My memory needs refreshing.
5. My batteries last only a few hours.
6. Airport security might ask you if you are carrying me.
7. I come in color and black & white.
8. I can play music for you.
9. I am a great traveler.
10. I have many keys, but can't open any doors.
11. I make millions of decisions every second.
12. I run on battery or power cord.
13. If you're not careful, I may get a virus.
14. I have a disk drive.
15. I heat up when I'm working.
16. My mouse doesn't eat cheese.
17. I like to sit on your lap.
18. If you drop me, I may break.
19. It's a big drag when I crash.
20. My name is a compound word.

Things

I AM A LAPTOP COMPUTER.

I am a Thing

1. Most people are happy to see me.
2. My "bow" doesn't go in your hair.
3. I know the whole spectrum.
4. My name combines a weather condition with a hair accessory.
5. Kermit sang a song about me.
6. I share my name with a type of trout.
7. Some people see me as a sign of good luck.
8. I describe the most colorful sherbet.
9. I know Roy G. Biv.
10. The world's largest natural bridge in Utah is named after me.
11. I am shaped in an arc.
12. People are always trying to find my end.
13. I need sun and rain to exist.
14. Sometimes I describe a wide assortment.
15. I am a natural phenomenon.
16. I appear in the sky.
17. Leprechauns use me as a hiding spot.
18. I am made up of seven different colors.
19. If calm comes before a storm, I come after.
20. Rumor has it you can find a pot of gold near me.

Things

I AM A RAINBOW.

20 Questions for girls

I am a Thing

1. I need to get charged up every day.
2. I've been called a public nuisance.
3. I have good hearing.
4. My ancestors often stayed by your bed or in the kitchen.
5. I can be a lifesaver in an emergency.
6. I'm not married, but I do have some nice rings.
7. I've been known to distract drivers.
8. I'm not a book, but I can text.
9. I can't sing, but I can carry a tune.
10. Despite my name, I have nothing to do with molecular biology.
11. I can go almost anywhere you go.
12. I'm usually banned on airplanes.
13. I can play games with you.
14. If you're crafty, you might decorate me with Swarovski crystals.
15. I can help your mother keep track of you.
16. The most common word that I hear is "Hello."
17. I might not always give you a great reception.
18. I fit in your back pocket.
19. In England, I'm mobile.
20. I might conk out on you.

12

Things

I AM A CELL PHONE.

I am a Thing

1. Most people either love me or hate me.
2. I am handmade.
3. You can make me at home if you have the right equipment.
4. My goal is to end up in your mouth.
5. I am almost always cold.
6. My "su" is not a girl.
7. I am usually made by highly-trained artisans.
8. I like it in the raw.
9. I have my own bar.
10. I don't have a bed, but I love to roll up with a nice bamboo mat.
11. My ginger doesn't know Thurston and Lovey.
12. I am a food.
13. There is something fishy about me.
14. I may come to dinner in a boat.
15. I'm usually eaten with sticks.
16. In California, I am green, pink and white.
17. My favorite beverage is sake.
18. You can find more of me in Japan than in Lapland.
19. The bento is my classic knife.
20. I have been stuffed and pressed.

Things

I AM SUSHI.

20 Questions for girls

I am a Thing

1. I can be found in the jungle
2. I'm sometimes found "in the middle" of a game of catch.
3. I'm often in Tarzan movies.
4. If I have bars, you can find me in a playground.
5. I am fun in a barrel.
6. Funny business is my business.
7. Sometimes I'm a sock.
8. I can be silly.
9. I love trees.
10. Scientists say that I'm closely related to humans.
11. I love to swing.
12. People think if I see, I do.
13. I am not found wild in the US.
14. I am popular at the zoo.
15. If you're handy with tools, you've probably used my wrench.
16. A curious one of my kind is famous.
17. I can hang from my tail and use it for balance.
18. In many countries, I'm kept as a pet.
19. Paul Frank uses my image a lot.
20. I think bananas are the best.

Things

I AM A MONKEY.

20 Questions for girls

I am a Thing

1. I am older than recorded history.
2. I can be hot or cold.
3. Adults seem to like me less than kids.
4. A female killer whale is my richest source.
5. I am sometimes flavored—or powdered.
6. Some say I can help you sleep when I'm warm.
7. I used to be delivered right to the doorstep.
8. I can be found on a farm.
9. The Romans mixed me with wine. Weird!
10. Coconuts are a natural source for me.
11. My mustaches are famous around the world.
12. I am a source of calcium.
13. I can come before or after chocolate.
14. I go well with pb & j.
15. Rumor has it that I'm good for building strong bones.
16. I am associated with Louis Pasteur.
17. Cows and soybeans produce me.
18. I like chocolate.
19. Babies need me.
20. I go well with cookies.

15

Things

I AM MILK.

20 Questions for girls

I am a Thing

1. My horses don't run.
2. I like a good tumble or two.
3. I am a popular Olympic event.
4. Before you were born, Nadia Comaneci was one of my champs.
5. I require balance.
6. I have bars of different sizes.
7. I have special camps.
8. I was started by the early Greeks.
9. Both males and females enjoy me.
10. I require you to be flexible.
11. I may be rhythmic.
12. My success relies on a regular routine.
13. I allow you to tumble around.
14. I have rings but no jewels.
15. Carly Patterson is one of my current stars.
16. My judges are not lawyers.
17. I am a good sport.
18. At the 2004 Olympics in Greece, my US women's team won a silver medal.
19. I have my own equipment.
20. I take place in a gymnasium.

16

Things

I AM GYMNASTICS.

I am a Thing

1. I am for kids.
2. I have money in my name.
3. If you move to a new town, I'll be in a new place.
4. I'm not an actor, but I do put on a good show.
5. I can be funny, entertaining and educational.
6. People tune in to me.
7. My name has five syllables.
8. I do my thing 24 hours a day.
9. My colors are orange and green.
10. I'm usually seen in your living room.
11. I can be animated or not.
12. You need cable to see me.
13. Some people think I'm *Unfabulous*.
14. I am named after a music machine.
15. To me, Zoey is number 101.
16. You are my audience.
17. I've got *Fairly OddParents*.
18. I help you soak up *SpongeBob SquarePants*.
19. My favorite boy's name is Nick.
20. I am a TV network.

Things

I AM NICKELODEON.

20 Questions for girls

I am a Thing

1. Some people get put under me.
2. I can be high- or low- powered.
3. I need to stay focused.
4. You won't find me at a playground.
5. You may find me at school.
6. Trust me, I can see things you can't.
7. My slide is not on the playground.
8. I make invisible things visible.
9. I'm an instrument that doesn't make music.
10. I take measurements.
11. I might make you squint.
12. I'm not contacts, but I do have a lens.
13. I help cure diseases.
14. I don't have a boyfriend, but I'm big on chemistry.
15. My light's just right.
16. I hunt diseases.
17. You can find me in a lab.
18. I make things look bigger.
19. Marie Curie used me.
20. You may see me at the Science Fair.

18

Things

I AM A MICROSCOPE.

I am a Thing

1. I can be a star attraction.
2. Don't confuse me with a fish.
3. I spend a lot of time in schools.
4. I can hold my breath for a really long time.
5. I'm an excellent swimmer, though I've never been on a team.
6. I'm a mammal.
7. Ranger Rick® has protected me for years.
8. Part of my anatomy sounds like part of my name.
9. I love fish.
10. I live in water.
11. I use sonar to navigate.
12. I'm supposed to be very smart.
13. My babies are called calves.
14. It seems I always have a smile on my face, but that's not really true.
15. I'm usually friendly to people.
16. I'm more like a whale than a shark.
17. I have a blowhole.
18. Sometimes I'm caught in tuna nets.
19. Flipper is the most famous of my kind.
20. It's believed that I've saved drowning sailors.

19

Things

I AM A DOLPHIN.

I am a Thing

1. I was invented in Belgium around 1870.
2. I am usually made of leather, metal and plastic.
3. Sometimes I have four wheels
4. I liked to be laced up.
5. People use me on sidewalks.
6. I usually have a toe stopper.
7. Some people wear kneepads when they use me.
8. I let people glide on wheels.
9. I am made by humans.
10. I am a great source of exercise.
11. You need coordination to use me.
12. You wear me on your feet.
13. I don't like to rock, but I do like to roll.
14. I'm kind of like a skateboard.
15. You can buy me in a toy store.
16. Both kids and adults can use me.
17. In a different version of me, you can glide on ice.
18. I used to come with a key.
19. Some people play a kind of hockey on me.
20. You can use me in rinks or in the park.

Things

I AM ROLLER SKATES.

I am a Thing

1. I'm a hard worker.
2. Lose your voice, and you'll sound like me.
3. I'm very particular about my shoes.
4. Please, get off my back.
5. I may wear a star on my forehead.
6. My socks won't come off.
7. I won't eat meat.
8. I can swim without lessons.
9. Sometimes you can bet on me.
10. I once delivered mail from St. Joseph to Sacramento.
11. I was painted 15,000 years ago.
12. China produces the most of me.
13. Sugar and carrots make me happy.
14. At the fair, you'll find me on the merry-go-round.
15. In England, I play polo.
16. I can be a real night*mare*.
17. I compete at the Summer Olympics.
18. Kids play me as a basketball shooting game.
19. Ford named a car after me.
20. Grab a saddle and I'll take you for a ride.

21

Things

I AM A HORSE.

I am a Thing

1. I'll give you a run for your money.
2. My sole has nothing to do with music.
3. I have two tongues, but no mouth.
4. I am an article of clothing.
5. Feet like me better than hands.
6. I never miss a good game of tennis.
7. Some boys wear me out quickly.
8. I come in pairs.
9. I'm not trying to hide, but I do like to sneak around.
10. I attend most sporting events.
11. Velcro can be a part of me.
12. I've never been to the jungle, but I'm familiar with Pumas.
13. I can be a real fashion statement.
14. I come in many different styles.
15. I need to fit to work.
16. I can have a high top.
17. I'm not chatty, but I will Converse with you.
18. I like leather and laces.
19. I can make your feet smell.
20. I come in many different colors.

22

Things

I AM SNEAKERS.

20 Questions for girls

I am a Thing

1. I can be very romantic.
2. I frequently attract insects.
3. My pistils don't shoot bullets.
4. I like to drink water.
5. If you talk flora and fauna you're talking me.
6. I am usually partly green in color.
7. I come in many colors and shapes.
8. I usually get picked first.
9. Petunia Pig and Daisy Duck might remind you of me.
10. I've been known to hang out in a wild bunch.
11. My bulbs don't light up.
12. In the 1960s, I was a kind of power.
13. Botanists study me.
14. I'm a rare treat in the desert.
15. Sometimes I smell.
16. Without me, gardens might not exist.
17. I'm a big part of Valentine's Day.
18. I don't like weeds any more than you do.
19. I rhyme with shower.
20. I share my name with one of Bambi's friends.

23

Things

I AM A FLOWER.

I am a Thing

1. I'm found in beds.
2. I'm an animal that doesn't eat.
3. Children like to hug me.
4. I'm cute and cuddly.
5. I sit around all day.
6. I'm usually very full.
7. I'm given as a gift.
8. My stuffing doesn't go with turkey.
9. If I'm a dog, I don't bark.
10. I'm warm and fuzzy.
11. I bring back memories.
12. I may be a bear to sleep with.
13. I can be a German import.
14. People of all ages enjoy me.
15. Kids take me on vacation.
16. You can buy me at the store.
17. I may be a purple dinosaur.
18. If I'm at the zoo, I'm in the gift shop.
19. In a pinch, I make a great pillow.
20. I've never been cut, but I'm full of stitches.

24

Things

I AM A STUFFED ANIMAL.

I am a Thing

1. I am usually not in the city.
2. I last about two weeks, more or less.
3. I'm mostly for tweens and teens.
4. No parents allowed! Except on special occasions.
5. I have rules you need to follow.
6. Sometimes I'm by a lake.
7. I'll help you make lots of new friends.
8. My beds are bunk.
9. Filofun™ is one of my favorite activities.
10. I have talent shows.
11. My kitchen is a mess hall.
12. I might make you artsy or crafty.
13. I love a good sing-along.
14. Summer is my season.
15. I make some people homesick.
16. You might make s'mores at me.
17. I have counselors.
18. I serve Bug Juice.
19. I usually have cabins.
20. I'm a kind of camp.

25

Things

I AM SUMMER CAMP.

I am a Thing

1. I hear lots of growling about my food.
2. I have tons of bars.
3. A lot of people who visit me think I smell.
4. Some of my crew work for peanuts.
5. Most people enjoy me when the weather's nice.
6. Some of my inhabitants love to monkey around.
7. You can learn a lot from me.
8. My star attractions aren't usually trained.
9. I see a lot of elementary school groups.
10. I usually contain hundreds of different habitats.
11. People come hither to see my friends slither.
12. If my inhabitants escape, things could get hairy.
13. Many animal rights activists are against me.
14. You'll see a lot of wild stuff if you visit me.
15. Sometimes a kiddy train runs through me.
16. You need a ticket to enter me.
17. You're not allowed to feed most of my inhabitants.
18. You'll have to do a lot of walking to fully enjoy me.
19. I can show you lions and tigers and bears. Oh my!
20. I can be found in San Diego, St. Louis, the Bronx and lots of other big cities.

26

Things

I AM THE ZOO.

I am a Thing

1. I come in many shapes and sizes.
2. I'm almost always painted.
3. I'm often made of wood.
4. Many people pass me on to their kids.
5. Hurricanes and earthquakes can destroy me.
6. You invite friends over to me.
7. I'm a great place for slumber parties.
8. I have at least four walls and a roof.
9. I have lots of rooms.
10. Sometimes I have a pool or tennis court.
11. You knock to enter me.
12. You might live in me.
13. I'm near a street.
14. When I'm an adjective, I'm a type of music.
15. I protect you from cold and rain.
16. People have used me for thousands of years.
17. I'm bigger than a car.
18. I have a mailbox nearby.
19. I can be made in a tree.
20. In Mexico, *soy una casa*.

Things

I AM A HOUSE.

I am a Thing

1. You may see boats from me.
2. I'm best to visit on a sunny day.
3. I don't like shoes much.
4. I'm good for picnics and barbeques.
5. I'm found around the world.
6. I'm always on the edge.
7. People come to me to fly kites.
8. Bring a towel when you visit me.
9. I see a lot of dogs and runners.
10. I'm sometimes linked with bums, bunnies and "combers."
11. My name rhymes with a type of fruit.
12. Sometimes I'm rocky.
13. A colored ball shares my name.
14. California and Hawaii are famous for me.
15. I have my own type of volleyball.
16. When you visit me, you might go swimming.
17. Some people head to me to get a tan.
18. Surfers like me.
19. You might build a sandcastle on me.
20. Visit me and collect seashells.

28

Things

I AM THE BEACH.

I am a Thing

1. My tickets won't go on your driving record.
2. I'm a source of entertainment.
3. I perform all over the world.
4. I sometimes describe an unorganized environment.
5. My net has nothing to do with computers.
6. Kids love me.
7. I travel a lot.
8. In Las Vegas, I have my own hotel.
9. Dr. Seuss® would put me behind Mr. Sneelock's store.
10. I have popcorn and peanuts.
11. My rings won't fit on your fingers.
12. I've got some high-fliers in my organization.
13. Some of my employees work for peanuts.
14. My top is big, but I have no bottom.
15. I'm full of animals, but I'm not a zoo.
16. I've been called the original freak show.
17. Tarzan could have worked for me.
18. My employees know how to clown around.
19. Monty Python got me flying.
20. Jumbo worked for me.

29

Things

I AM THE CIRCUS.

20 Questions for girls

I am a Thing

1. You can find me in most major cities.
2. The public supports me.
3. But I can also be private.
4. Sometimes I'm just for kids.
5. I like to put things on display.
6. People pay to see me.
7. I'm educational.
8. I store precious objects.
9. My gardens are well kept.
10. My boss is called a curator.
11. I'm popular for field trips.
12. I often have a gift shop and a café.
13. I've existed for centuries.
14. I can specialize in lots of different things: natural history, science, TV & film and more!
15. I am usually in a specially-designed building.
16. Sometimes I'm modern. Sometimes I'm old.
17. My walls are meant to be decorated.
18. People usually whisper in me, but I'm not a library.
19. *Mona Lisa* lives in me.
20. If you like art, you might like me.

30

Things

I AM A MUSEUM.

I am a Thing

1. I'm found all over the world.
2. I start and end with a ring.
3. I usually take a break in the summer.
4. When I'm slang, I can be old or new.
5. I'm usually closed on weekends.
6. I'm a six-letter word.
7. I'm not easy, but sometimes I'm elementary.
8. You'll see your mates in me.
9. I can be a group of fish.
10. I can be public or private.
11. I only go up to 12.
12. I put on dances and plays.
13. I'm not a snob, but I've got class.
14. Sometimes I have a mascot.
15. I'll teach you a thing or two.
16. I've got spirit, yes I do. I've got spirit, how 'bout you?
17. I'm not an office, but I do have desks.
18. Mary's lamb followed her to me.
19. When you finish me, you graduate.
20. Because of me, you've got homework.

31

Things

I AM A SCHOOL.

I am a Thing

1. Spring in Washington, D.C. wouldn't be the same without me.
2. I'm red, but I'm no book.
3. I'm a type of blossom.
4. I share my name with a tomato and a pepper.
5. The wood of my tree is prized.
6. I am a flavor of Starburst®.
7. I am a member of the rose family.
8. I grow on trees.
9. I am small and round.
10. I make a great pie.
11. My bomb packs a bang on the 4th.
12. Do you think Billy Boy can bake me?
13. I don't have arms, but I do have pits.
14. If I'm organic, I cost more.
15. I can be sour or sweet.
16. I was in Greece before 300 B.C.
17. Sometimes, life is just a bowl of me.
18. I'm a type of fruit.
19. I rhyme with fairy.
20. Supposedly, George Washington chopped down my tree.

32

Things

I AM A CHERRY.

ABOUT THE AUTHOR

Bob Moog, co-founder of University Games and publisher of Spinner Books, has been creating games and puzzles and the like since childhood. He tormented his four younger siblings with quizzes, conundrums and physical and mental challenges during the 1960s. Now, he introduces the Spinner Books for Kids™ series, hoping it will challenge and puzzle you as much as his early "work" did his family 40 years ago.

Moog is the author of several other puzzle/game and children's books, including *Gummy Bear Goes to Camp*, *Symbol Simon*®, *30 Second Mysteries*™ and *Secret Identities*™.

Enjoy Spinner Books?

30 Second Mysteries
For 2 Teams
Ages 8 and Up
Follow the clues to crack the case!

Kids Battle the Grown-Ups
Who really knows more...the kids or the grown-ups?

TOTALLY GROSS!
THE GAME
of science

new edition!
20 Questions for kids
play the classic game of people, places and things!
ages 7 to 12
for 2 to 10 players

Get the Original Games!

Find these games and more at your nearest toy store.